AV

LIONEL MESSI

Jon M. Fishman

Lerner Publications ◆ Minneapolis

Lerner Publications Company
A division of Lerner Publishing Group, Inc.
241 First Avenue North
Minneapolis, MN 55401 USA

For reading levels and more information, look up this title at www.lernerbooks.com.

Main body text set in Albany Std 15/22. Typeface provided by Agfa.

Library of Congress Cataloging-in-Publication Data

Names: Fishman, Jon M., author.
Title: Lionel Messi / Jon M. Fishman.
Description: Minneapolis, MN : Lerner Publications, 2017. | Includes bibliographical
    references and index. | Audience: Age 7–11. | Audience: Grade 4 to 6.
Identifiers: LCCN 2016055020 (print) | LCCN 2016055915 (ebook) | ISBN
    9781512434545 (lb : alk. paper) | ISBN 9781512456189 (pb : alk. paper) | ISBN
    9781512450903 (eb pdf)
Subjects: LCSH: Messi, Lionel, 1987-—Juvenile literature. | Soccer players—
    Argentina—Biography—Juvenile literature.
Classification: LCC GV942.7.M398 F57 2017 (print) | LCC GV942.7.M398 (ebook) |
    DDC 796.334092 [B] —dc23

LC record available at https://lccn.loc.gov/2016055020

Manufactured in the United States of America
1-42103-25397-3/23/2017

CONTENTS

BALL

Lionel Messi controls the ball in a match against Sevilla FC.

Me-ssi! Me-ssi! Me-ssi!

If you go to a soccer match in Barcelona, Spain, there's a good chance you'll hear this chant from the stands. The fans are cheering for Futbol Club (FC) Barcelona's Lionel Messi, one of the best soccer players in the world. Messi showed off his incredible talent in a **La Liga** match on November 6, 2016.

FC Barcelona faced Sevilla FC. Trailing 1–0, Barcelona players raced down the **pitch** with the ball. Denis Suarez passed to Neymar. Neymar danced toward the goal. He cut to his right. He moved to the front of the goal as the Sevilla defense closed in for the **tackle**. At the last second, Neymar flicked the ball to Messi's left foot.

Messi races toward the ball during the match against Sevilla FC.

Messi didn't hesitate. He didn't stop the ball to line up the perfect shot. Instead, he smacked the ball as it bounced toward him and sent it streaking into the net. Goal! It was Messi's 500th goal in 592 games with Barcelona.

Later in the game, Messi raced to the net again. The Sevilla defense blocked his path. Messi passed to teammate Luis

Most soccer players prefer to kick with one leg. They call this their stronger leg. Messi's left leg is his stronger leg. But he can also score with his right. He has one of strongest weaker legs in the world.

Suarez. Suarez sent the ball zooming into the goal. The teammates hugged as the crowd roared. Messi's **assist** helped Barcelona win the game, 2–1.

In 2009, Messi won the FIFA Ballon d'Or award as the top player in men's soccer. Then he won the award three more times in a row. Cristiano Ronaldo took it home in 2013 and 2014. But Messi was back on top for 2015. "It's incredible [that] this is my fifth [FIFA Ballon d'Or award]," Messi said. "It's much more than anything I've dreamed of as a kid."

Messi poses with his 2015 FIFA Ballon d'Or award.

Rosario is one of the largest cities in Argentina

Lionel Messi was born on June 24, 1987, in Rosario, Argentina. Rosario is about 186 miles (300 kilometers) northwest of the nation's capital, Buenos Aires.

In Argentina, soccer is a big deal. There are soccer fields all around the country. People begin playing as soon as they can walk and enjoy the game until old age forces them off the pitch. Argentina's national team won the World Cup in 1978 and 1986.

Argentina's national team celebrates winning the 1978 World Cup.

Lionel loved the sport. He was good, but he didn't stand out on his youth team in Rosario. "I don't think anybody expects their friend will become the best player in the world," said childhood teammate Lucas Scaglia. Newell's Old Boys, as the team was called, lost only one game during a four-year stretch. Since most of the players were born in 1987, fans called them the Machine of '87.

CAPITAL · **PASIVN** · Domingo 3 de septiembre de 2000

hoy presentamos
lionel andrés messi

Lionel Messi es jugador de la décima división y el enganche del equipo. Como chico, no sólo es una de las promesas de la cantera leprososa, sino que tiene un futuro enorme porque, a pesar de su estatura, él se las arregla para pasar a uno, dos, gambetear, hacer goles pero, por sobre todas las cosas, se divierte con la redonda y hoy se presenta en sociedad.

Un ídolo: Dos, mi papá Jorge y mi padrino Claudio.
Un técnico: Todos los que tuve, porque de todos aprendí cosas (Gabriel, Morales, Domínguez, Vecchio y Coria).
Un preparador físico: Pablo Sánchez.
Un jugador: Dos, mi hermano y mi primo.
Un equipo: Newell's.
Un hobbie: Escuchar música.
Un tipo de música: Cuarteto y cumbia.
Un programa de TV: Primicias.
Una revista: Pasión Rojinegra.
Un libro: La Biblia.
Una película: Cuidado, "bebé suelto".
Otro deporte: Handboll.
Una modelo: Nicole Neumann.
Una comida: Pollo con salsa.
Una materia: Lengua.
Un estudio: Profesor de educación física.
Un objetivo: Terminar la secundaria.
Una meta: Llegar a primera.

Una alegría: Cuando salimos campeones 10ma.
Una tristeza: El fallecimiento de mi abuel
Una ilusión: Jugar en la primera de Newe
Un recuerdo: Cuando mi abuela me llevó p mera vez a jugar al fútbol.
Un sueño: Jugar en la selección.
Una anécdota: Cuando viajamos a Perú mos campeones.
Humildad: Es lo que un ser humano no de der nunca.
Las selecciones juveniles: Me gustaría p tegrarlas.
Expectativas para este año: Poder salir c de nuevo.
La familia: Mi papá Jorge, mi mamá Ce hermanos Rodrigo, Natalia y Marisol.
Los amigos: Gracias a Dios tengo much nos, nombrarlos sería olvidarme de al
¿Qué representa Newell's en tu vida? To ximo.

un leprosito que se las tra

Nombre y apellido: Lionel Andrés Messi.
Fecha de nacimiento: 24-06-87.
Lugar: Rosario.
Apodo: Leo.

Puesto: Enganche.
Principal característica: Buena gambeta.
Trayectoria: Grandoli y Newell's.
División: Décima división.

Lionel was featured in a Rosario newspaper in 2000 when he was 12 years old. He is wearing a jersey for Newell's Old Boys.

Lionel's agreement to sign up with Barcelona was written and signed on a napkin in 2000.

As Lionel grew, so did his soccer skills. Before long, his lightning-quick feet caught the attention of fans and **scouts**. But then a huge problem arose. When he was nine years old, Lionel stopped growing.

Lionel was lacking a **hormone** in his body that helped him grow. It could be treated, but the treatment cost as much as $1,000 a month. At first, Newell's Old Boys helped pay the bills. But the team decided it was too expensive.

Scouts from FC Barcelona had seen Lionel play. He was small but also amazingly quick and talented. They offered to pay for Lionel's hormone treatment if he would sign up with the team. He would also have to move to Spain.

When he was thirteen years old, Lionel moved with his father to Spain. Lionel lived at La Masia, a place where young athletes live and learn the game. The treatments worked, and he grew to 5 feet 7 (1.7 meters). He also greatly improved as a player. He played his first game for Barcelona at the age of 16. In May 2005, he became the youngest player to ever score a goal for the team. He was on his way to stardom.

Messi (left) fights for the ball during a training session at La Masia in 2005.

Messi and teammate Ronaldinho celebrate a goal during a match in 2005.

Messi warms up before a game in 2016.

Do you get enough exercise? Do you think you could pass a test to prove it? Lionel Messi always keeps his body in top shape. But FC Barcelona makes all of its players prove their fitness each year. Before the start of the season, Messi reports to the

Staying in world-class shape is a lot of work. But it's easier when you've spent a lifetime playing sports. "As a child I always had a ball on me. . . ." Lionel said. "More than once I slept with my ball."

team's headquarters for a series of tests. First, doctors put **sensors** on his body. Then Messi runs on a treadmill. The sensors measure his heartbeat, breathing, and other signs from his body. Doctors also check his weight and the movement of his joints.

On the practice pitch, Messi works on his speed. He does

Messi (center) moves the ball between two defenders during an FC Barcelona training session.

drills that improve how fast he can run forward and backward. Other drills focus on running sideways and at odd angles. These workouts improve his strength, balance, and quickness.

Messi participates in a training session in 2016.

As soon as a match ends, Messi starts thinking about the next one. "We play a lot of games in a very short space of time, so I think it's important to always look forward and never backward," he said. He imagines how the next team will try to stop him. He pictures himself succeeding, and then he tries to make it happen.

Another big part of his success is his diet. In 2014, Messi gave up some of the foods that he loves, such as pizza. These days, he goes for more healthful options. Fresh fruits and vegetables, whole grains, and nuts and seeds are on the menu. He also drinks plenty of water. He doesn't eat much meat. And he always stays away from sugary foods.

Messi jumps to head the ball during FC Barcelona training.

SPREADING GOODWILL

Messi poses with Antonella Roccuzzo at the 2014 FIFA Ballon d'Or awards ceremony.

Messi is an international superstar.

But he doesn't live like one. Messi and his girlfriend, Antonella Roccuzzo, have a growing family. Their first son, Thiago, was born in November 2012. Mateo, the couple's second son, was born in September 2015.

After a match, Messi usually heads home to be with his family. He might play games with his kids. Other nights, he drifts off to sleep early with the TV on in the background.

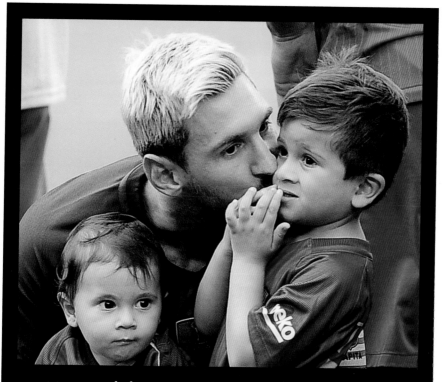

Messi with his sons, Thiago (*right*) and Mateo, before a match in 2016

Connected to the Ball

Messi admires National Basketball Association (NBA) superstar Stephen Curry of the Golden State Warriors. He noticed something about the way Curry plays. Curry seems to know where the ball is going to go before it happens. According to Messi, it's almost as if Curry's mind and body have a connection to the basketball.

Stephen Curry

That's the way Messi tries to play too. He knows where the ball will be, and he races to those spots with bursts of speed no one else can match.

Curry and Messi haven't met in person. But the soccer star is hoping that will change soon. The two megastars began a long-distance friendship by exchanging signed jerseys.

He plays to win on and off the pitch. Messi plays *EA Sports FIFA 16* online with his friends and teammates. The soccer video game is popular around the world. It must be even more fun to play when you're on the cover. Messi has been featured on the game's cover four years in a row.

Messi stands beside an image of the cover of *EA Sports FIFA 13*.

Messi was the first Barcelona player to be named a United Nations Children's Fund (UNICEF) goodwill ambassador.

unicef

unicef

Messi also appears in advertisements for companies such as Adidas. Money from these companies has helped make Messi rich. *Forbes* magazine said he earned $28 million from advertisements in 2016. He also made more than $53 million playing soccer. That made him the second-highest paid athlete in the world! Only Cristiano Ronaldo makes more money.

Messi waves to fans after being named a UNICEF goodwill ambassador.

Messi uses some of his money to help others. In 2007, the Leo Messi Foundation began helping children in Argentina and Spain. The foundation works with hospitals and other groups to give children a better chance at success. UNICEF honored Messi in 2010. The group named him a goodwill ambassador. In that role, Messi travels around the world. He spreads UNICEF's message that all children deserve a chance to succeed.

CHAMPION OF
CHAMPIONS

Messi hoists a trophy as he celebrates a 2015 FC Barcelona win.

Messi hoists a trophy as he celebrates a 2015 FC Barcelona win.

Lionel Messi has had an incredible run of success in European soccer.
He helped FC Barcelona win the La Liga championship eight times. Messi and his teammates won the **Champions League**

in 2006, 2009, 2011, and 2015. In 2014, he became the all-time leading goal scorer in La Liga.

The 2016–2017 La Liga season began much as the previous seasons had for Messi. By mid-November, he led the league in goals. FC Barcelona had won eight matches in 11 chances. All seemed well with the Spanish soccer world.

Messi (left) goes up against German goalkeeper Kevin Trapp during a match in 2017.

Messi hasn't had as much success with the Argentina national team as he's had with other teams. At the 2016 Olympics in Rio de Janeiro, Brazil, Argentina beat Algeria, 2–1. But a loss to Cristiano Ronaldo's Portugal and a draw with Honduras knocked Argentina out of the Olympics.

But Messi's future on the team was uncertain. Messi had agreed to a **contract** in 2014 that paid him more than $50 million a year. It made him one of the highest-paid soccer players in the world. But that contract was due to end in 2018.

Would Messi leave the team that had brought him to Europe from Argentina? Would he abandon the city that made him rich beyond anything he could have imagined?

European soccer powers such as Manchester United lined up to make him an offer he couldn't refuse. But wherever he plays, Lionel Messi is sure to be the best player on the pitch.

Messi celebrates a goal during a 2017 game.

All-Star Stats

Messi can do it all on a soccer pitch. He makes pinpoint passes and always seems to know where he needs to be to help his team. But he's best known for his incredible ability to score goals. La Liga is full of scoring superstars, but Messi stands out from the pack.

Most Goals in a La Liga Season

Goals	Player	Season
50	Lionel Messi	2011–2012
48	Cristiano Ronaldo	2014–2015
46	Lionel Messi	2012–2013
46	Cristiano Ronaldo	2011–2012
43	Lionel Messi	2014–2015
40	Cristiano Ronaldo	2010–2011
40	Luis Suarez	2015–2016
38	Hugo Sanchez	1989–1990
38	Telmo Zarra	1950–1951
35	Baltazar	1988–1989

Source Notes

7   Dermot Corrigan, "Lionel Messi Wins 2015 Ballon d'Or ahead of Cristiano Ronaldo, Neymar," *ESPN FC*, January 11, 2016, http://www.espnfc.us/blog/fifa/243/post/2784555/lionel-messi-wins-2015-ballon-dor-ahead-of-ronaldo-neymar

10 Liviu Bird, "Ex-Teammate, La Masia Coach Recall Lionel Messi's Early Days, Persona," *Sports Illustrated*, June 4, 2015, http://www.si.com/planet-futbol/2015/06/04/lionel-messi-champions-league-final-barcelona

15 Grant Wahl, "American Dream," *Sports Illustrated*, accessed November 13, 2016, http://www.si.com/longform/2016/lionel-messi-copa-america-argentina-barcelona

16 Andrew Murray, "Lionel Messi: I'm Not the Sort of Guy Who Shouts and Screams before a Match," *FourFourTwo*, April 21, 2015, http://www.fourfourtwo.com/us/features/lionel-messi-im-not-sort-guy-who-shouts-and-screams-match

Glossary

assist: a pass that helps a teammate score a goal

Champions League: a yearly competition between Europe's top soccer teams

contract: an agreement between an athlete and a team that determines a player's salary and time with the team

drills: exercises used to improve athletic skill

hormone: a substance made in the body that aids growth

La Liga: Spain's top professional soccer league

pitch: a soccer field

scouts: people who judge the skills of athletes

sensors: devices that measure and record physical things such as heartbeats

tackle: take the ball away from an opponent

Further Information

Braun, Eric. *Stephen Curry*. Minneapolis: Lerner Publications, 2017.

Doeden, Matt. *Cristiano Ronaldo*. Minneapolis: Lerner Publications, 2017.

FC Barcelona
https://www.fcbarcelona.com

FIFA
http://www.fifa.com

FIFA World Cup Russia 2018
http://www.fifa.com/worldcup

Morreale, Marie. *Lionel Messi*. New York: Children's Press, 2016.

Index

Photo Acknowledgments

The images in this book are used with the permission of: © Visionhaus/Corbis Sport/
Getty Images, p. 2 (background); © iStockphoto.com/iconeer, p. 4 (gold star page
numbers); Mutsu Kawamori/AFLO/Newscom, pp. 4–5; © Aitor Alcalde/Getty Images,
p. 6; © Mike Hewitt - FIFA/Getty Images, p. 7; © iStockphoto.com/ozzmancometh53,
p. 8; © Javier Heinzmann/STR/Getty Images, p. 10; Mirrorpix/Newscom, p. 9; AP
Photo/Manu Fernandez, pp. 11, 17; © LLUIS GENE/AFP/Getty Images, pp. 12, 13;
© PAU BARRENA/AFP/Getty Images, p. 14; Francesc Adelantado/ZUMA Press/
Newscom, p. 15; REUTERS/Alamy Stock Photo, p. 16, 22; 23; Marcio Machado/
ZUMA Wire/Alamy Live News, p. 18; © Joan Cros Garcia - Corbis/Getty Images, p. 19;
© Jeff Siner/Charlotte Observer/TNS via Getty Images, p. 20; TONI ALBIR/EPA/
Newscom, p. 21; Barcelona V Juventus/ZUMA Press/Newscom, p. 24; © PHILIPPE
LOPEZ/AFP/Getty Images, p. 25; Quique Garcia/EPA/Newscom, p. 27.

Cover: © Visionhaus/Corbis Sport/Getty Images.